Julie Eisenhower's Cookbook for Children

Doubleday and Co., Inc.

A special note of thanks to
Mrs. Rosalyn Volpert Fox
for her aid in testing
many of the recipes; and
to Cindy Vanden Heuvel
for her outstanding
secretarial assistance.

Illustrated by Don Moldroski

Introduction

How many times have you asked your mother or father "What's for dinner?" Wouldn't it be fun to choose the meal and plan it yourself, and sometimes even surprise other members of your family or your friends? This cookbook is written especially for you. There are over 100 simple recipes to try, many of them from young people. You will discover what others enjoy eating when you prepare dishes like "Liz Ann's Butterscotch Brownies" and "Michael's Hot Porridge." And you will learn a new language, the language of the kitchen: words like *simmer* and *sprinkle; dot* and *drizzle!*

If you have a good time with this cookbook, I will be happy because that is the reason I wrote it. I hope you will agree with me that it is fun to be able to make a dish easily and then find out it tastes good too! With this cookbook, if it is raining outside and you wish it were snowing, you can make a snowflake cake (p.71). Do you like to build things? Pretend you are constructing a six-story building as you prepare "Six-Layer Dinner" (p.38). Or search for gold (fruit) in a mountain of yogurt (p.10). There is an unexplored world of tastes and smells and textures for the new cook. Once you start, you will become bold and add all kinds of delicious ingredients to the recipes that I never dreamed of.

To make this cookbook very special, I asked some of the people (and even a bird) you see on television and read about to share their favorite recipes. You can pretend you are eating dinner on a clattering train, rolling through the mountains of

Shanghai when you make Mrs. Billy Graham's "Tsao Fan" (fried rice with ham and scrambled eggs). Lynda Johnson Robb's daughters, Cindy and Kathy, tell you how to make Christmas decorations out of pretend dough. Big Bird of Sesame Street, the real Maria of *The Sound of Music,* Mister Rogers and many more introduce you to their favorite foods.

The only keys to the world of cooking are enthusiasm, inventiveness and a willingness to clean up pots and pans and measuring utensils as you cook and to have an adult help you when you use the stove and sharp knives. As you discover that cooking does not have to mean a hot, dirty room or hard work but rather nice smells, lots of stirring, sometimes squishing and mixing and later soapsuds, you will want to get to know the kitchen better. This cookbook is just a first step to an adventure which will last as long as you live.

Postscript to Parents

Cooking can be extraordinarily creative and a source of satisfaction throughout life. I do not believe a child who is willing to learn can be introduced to the kitchen too early. The purpose of my *Children's Cookbook* is to provide simple and appealing recipes so children and their parents can enjoy cooking together. And although the recipes are easy to prepare, they are not boring. For example, opening one can may be unexciting but opening three — blithely mixing the contents together as the cans quickly fill up yet another kitchen garbage bag — is fun, especially when the result is as tasty as "One-Two-Three Soup" (p. 23).

With rare exceptions no recipe takes more than fifteen minutes to prepare. There are several reasons. First, a great many of the recipes are from my personal file and reflect my style of cooking. After six years of marriage and being on my own in the kitchen, I am convinced that one can create delicious, even unusual and elegant meals in a limited amount of time. Secondly, parents who prepare all the meals and innumerable snacks spend hours in the kitchen daily. Since supervision in using knives and stoves is necessary when children cook, I wanted the recipes in this book to be a joy to make and not add to the already existing household pressures.

I think the kitchen is one of the best places for family togetherness. If you are eager to eliminate turned-up noses at suppertime or a child rushing through his meal or squirming with boredom once his ice cream is gone, then involve him in deciding *what* to prepare; help him realize that cooking is a labor of love, and that time and fun go into preparing "Daddy's Favorite Steak Sauce."

There is enjoyment and excitement waiting for the child in the kitchen if we just open the door for him.

Cooking Terms to Help You Along the Way

Bake — Cook in oven.

Beat — Mix very fast with a spoon or fork, or round and round with a rotary beater.

Blend — Mix 2 or more ingredients until smooth.

Boil — Cook until liquid is so hot it bubbles.

Broil — Cook directly under heating unit in range, or over hot coals.

Chop — Cut into pieces with a knife or chopper.

Cream — Beat until fluffy and creamy.

Cube — Cut into ¼- to ½-inch squares.

Dot — Drop bits of butter or cheese over the entire surface of the food you are cooking.

Drain — Pour off liquid.

Grate — Rub cheese, carrots, etc. against grater to cut into small flakelike pieces. Be sure to have an adult help you when using the grater.

Grease — Spread bottom and sides of pan with shortening.

Melt — Heat until liquid.

Mince — Chop or cut into tiny pieces.

Mound — Heap food into a mountain shape.

Peel — Pull off outer skin, as from an orange or banana.

Sift — Put through flour sifter or fine sieve.

Simmer — Cook over very low heat until liquid is hot but not bubbling.

Stir — Mix round and round with spoon.

Toss — Mix ingredients lightly.

Whip — Beat with rotary egg beater or electric mixer to add air.

Table of Contents

Good Morning Breakfasts

Doughnut Surprise

serves 4

4 plain doughnuts
8 teaspoons butter
8 teaspoons brown sugar
8 teaspoons shredded coconut

Slice doughnuts sideways.

Butter each half and sprinkle with 1 teaspoon brown sugar and 1 teaspoon coconut.

Toast under broiler at 350 degrees for about 5 minutes.

Gold in the Mountain

A fun and different way to begin the day.
serves 1

1 cup yogurt
½ cup of your favorite fruit
1 tablespoon toasted wheat germ

In a cereal bowl, make a mountain of yogurt. Hide pieces of your favorite fruit inside the mountain — cherries, pineapple, peaches, grapes, bananas, melon.

Sprinkle wheat germ on top.

Michael's Porridge

serves 4

3 cups water
1 cup dried apricots
1 teaspoon salt
1⅓ cups Instant Quaker Oats
Cinnamon
Honey
Cream or milk

Bring water to a boil and add apricots.
Cook for 5 minutes over low heat.

Add salt and oatmeal to boiling water with fruit
and cook for 1 minute.

Cover pan and remove from heat.

After 3 minutes, spoon into cereal bowls and top
with cinnamon, honey and cream or milk.

Cheddar Muffin Breakfast

serves 4

4 cornbread muffins
8 slices cheddar cheese

Slice muffins in half crosswise.

Top each muffin half with a thin slice of cheese and
place under broiler until cheese melts.

Get-Up-and-Go-Orange Drink

serves 2

1 egg
½ cup milk
1 (6-ounce) can frozen orange juice

Place all ingredients in blender and whip until smooth.

Ham and Eggs

serves 4

1 (4½-ounce) can deviled ham
8 soda crackers, crushed
4 eggs

Mix deviled ham with cracker crumbs. Place 2 tablespoons
in each of 4 muffin tins. Pat some of the ham partially
up the sides of the tins.

Drop eggs on top of ham.

Cut piece of aluminum foil a little larger than the muffin
pan. Cut small hole in center to allow the steam to escape.
Place aluminum foil loosely over eggs so they will stay
tender while baking.

Bake in 325-degree preheated oven until eggs are
firm — about 15 minutes.

Scoop ham and eggs out of muffin pans
onto 4 slices of buttered toast.

Serve plain or sprinkle with chopped chives or parsley.

Quick and Cool Breakfast

A breakfast which takes one minute to make.
serves 2

1 ripe cantaloupe
1 cup plain yogurt
2 cherries

Cut melon in half and remove seeds.

Fill center of each half melon with ½ cup yogurt.

Top with cherry.

Banana Shake

My favorite snack — any time of the day.
serves 1

1 ripe banana
1 teaspoon vanilla
1 cup plain yogurt

Place all ingredients in blender for one minute.

Pour into tall glass and serve.

Bananas in a Blanket

serves 4

4 bananas, peeled
4 thin slices boiled ham
4 teaspoons margarine

Wrap each banana with ham slice, top with margarine
and place in baking dish.
Bake 8 minutes at 425 degrees, or until ham is light brown.

French Toast

serves 2

2 eggs
2 tablespoons wheat germ
2 tablespoons water
1 teaspoon vanilla
1 teaspoon sugar
2 tablespoons oil
4 pieces cracked wheat bread

In small bowl beat eggs; then stir in wheat germ,
water, vanilla and sugar.

Heat oil in skillet over medium heat.

Dip each bread slice into egg mixture.

Place in frying pan and cook until bread is
brown on both sides.

Serve with butter and syrup.

Salads

St. Patrick's Day Shamrock Pears

*But these beautiful green pears with a mint flavor are
good any time of the year.*
serves 4

1 jar mint jelly
2 drops green food coloring
4 canned pear halves
4 lettuce leaves
4 scoops cottage cheese

Put jelly in saucepan and stir over low heat
until jelly melts. Stir in food coloring.

Dip each pear half in jelly, coating it green.

Place pear half on lettuce leaf and fill center
with cottage cheese.

Apple Salad

serves 2

1 apple, sliced
1 celery stalk, sliced
2 tablespoons pineapple tidbits
2 tablespoons mayonnaise
2 tablespoons Swiss cheese, shredded
1 tablespoon walnuts, chopped

In a bowl, mix all the ingredients together.

Serve on lettuce leaves.

Easy Four-Bean Salad

A wonderful salad which keeps in the refrigerator for days.
serves 4 to 6

1 (1-pound) can red kidney beans
1 (1-pound) can lima beans
1 (1-pound) can wax beans
1 (1-pound) can French-cut green beans
1 large onion
½ cup sugar
½ cup oil
½ cup cider vinegar
½ teaspoon pepper
½ teaspoon salt

Drain and rinse kidney beans.
Drain lima, wax and green beans.

Mix the four kinds of beans.

Slice onion, separate slices into rings
and add to bean mixture.

Combine sugar, oil, vinegar, pepper and salt.

Pour over bean-onion mixture and toss.

Refrigerate several hours or overnight.

Bananas in the Jungle

It's fun to look for the bananas in the green jungle.
serves 4

½ head lettuce
10 raw spinach leaves
1 ripe banana
4 tablespoons Russian dressing

Wash lettuce and spinach leaves;
tear into bite-size pieces.

Pat leaves dry with paper towels.

Slice banana into the salad and toss with your
favorite Russian dressing.

Fabulous Confetti Salad Dressing

serves 6

⅓ cup sugar
⅓ cup lemon juice
½ cup salad oil
1½ teaspoons salt
1 tablespoon minced onion
2 tablespoons finely chopped green pepper
2 tablespoons finely chopped pimiento
2 tablespoons finely chopped celery

Place all ingredients in a jar and shake well. Chill.
Shake again before serving.

Out-of-this-World Chicken Salad

serves 6

2 (11-ounce) cans Mandarin oranges
¼ cup salted almonds
1 banana
2 cups chicken cut into cubes
½ pound sharp cheddar cheese, cubed
½ cup mayonnaise
12 pineapple rings

Drain orange sections.

Chop almonds into small pieces.

Slice banana into thin, round pieces.

Mix oranges, almonds, banana slices, chicken, cheese
and mayonnaise in a bowl.

Place 2 pineapple rings on each plate.

Mound chicken salad on top of pineapple
rings and serve.

Skinny Salad Dressing

A low-calorie dressing everyone will like.
serves 4

1 cup plain low-fat yogurt
1 teaspoon honey
2 teaspoons lemon juice

Mix well. Serve over fruit salad.

Salads

Before-You-Go-To-Bed Cucumbers

These cucumbers taste best when they spend the night in the refrigerator. They are so good you'll want them for breakfast, lunch and dinner.
serves 4 to 6

4 peeled and sliced cucumbers
1 cup Wishbone Italian salad dressing
3 tablespoons white vinegar
4 tablespoons sugar
1 teaspoon pepper

Slice cucumbers into rounds.

Mix dressing, vinegar, sugar and pepper.

Pour over cucumbers.

Place in refrigerator before you go to bed.

Next day serve on bed of lettuce.

Sergeant Moaney's Salad Dressing

Sergeant Moaney likes sweet salad dressing
serves 2

3 tablespoons vegetable oil
1 tablespoon vinegar
1 tablespoon catsup
½ teaspoon sugar
¼ teaspoon salt
⅛ teaspoon pepper

Place all ingredients in bottle and shake well.

Soups

Snowflake Soup

This snow can fall on any soup.
serves 3

1 can potato soup
1 soup can milk
½ cup popped corn
3 tablespoons grated Swiss cheese

Mix soup and milk in saucepan and stir until hot.

Pour soup into bowls.

Float popcorn (snow) and shredded cheese
on top of each bowl of soup.

Count-to-Ten Egg Drop Soup

It's fun to watch the egg turn into ribbons
as you count to ten.
serves 4

2 (10-ounce) cans chicken broth
2 soup cans of water
2 eggs
2 teaspoons soy sauce

Place soup and water in saucepan and heat to boiling.

In small bowl, beat eggs and soy sauce (with rotary beater).

Pour eggs into hot broth and stir while you count to 10.

Serve immediately.

One-Two-Three Soup

Just three cans to open for a quick, delicious soup.
serves 4

1 can tomato soup
1 can green pea soup
1 can beef consommé
1 teaspoon chopped chives, if desired

Empty all three cans into saucepan.

Heat until hot, stirring constantly.

Sprinkle with chopped chives before serving.

Pink Panther Soup

I could eat this soup every day of the week.
serves 6

2 (1-pound) cans tomatoes
Juice of one lemon
¼ teaspoon celery salt
¼ teaspoon curry powder
16 ounces plain yogurt

Drain tomatoes.

Place all ingredients in blender and blend until smooth.

Put blender in refrigerator for at least 1 hour before serving.

Blushing Corn Chowder

serves 2

1 can tomato soup
1 soup can of milk
1 teaspoon sugar
½ cup cream-style corn

Empty soup and milk into saucepan.

Stir in sugar and corn.

Heat until hot; do not boil.

"You Better Eat Your Spinach, Soupy"

Most of my young friends love this combination!
serves 2

1 can chicken or turkey soup
½ cup cooked spinach

Heat soup and spinach together and serve.

Sandwiches

Skyhigh Sandwich

When you make this sandwich, let your imagination run wild.
serves 1

Bun or brown bread
2 tablespoons Russian dressing
2 tablespoons pickle relish
2 slices bologna
1 hard-cooked egg, sliced
Lettuce, tomato slice, green pepper
1 slice your favorite cheese
2 slices turkey
2 slices bacon

Spread bread with Russian dressing and pickle relish and stack all other ingredients on top.

Finish with other slice of bread or bun.

Soup Sandwich

For cold days when you can't decide between
soup or a sandwich.
serves 6

1 can tomato soup
1 cup shredded or cubed cheddar cheese
6 pieces whole wheat toast

Place tomato soup in saucepan.

Add cheese and cook until cheese melts.

Pour over toasted bread.

Crabby but Good

When you feel like mixing lots of ingredients together.
serves 4

1 (8-ounce) package cream cheese
1 (6-ounce) can crab meat, drained
1 teaspoon Worcestershire sauce
1 teaspoon instant onion
1 tablespoon lemon juice
½ teaspoon salt
4 English muffins
8 slices cheese
2 tomatoes, each cut in 4 slices

Mix cream cheese, crab, Worcestershire sauce,
instant onion, lemon juice, and salt.

Spread mixture on muffin halves.

Place 1 cheese and tomato slice on each muffin.

Bake at 350 degrees for 15 minutes.

Chris' Favorite

My friend Chris could eat this every day, and usually does!
serves 1

2 slices pumpernickel bread
Mayonnaise
Lettuce leaf
2 slices crisp bacon
4 tablespoons peanut butter

Spread 1 slice of bread with mayonnaise.

Place lettuce leaf and bacon slices on top.

Spread other slice with peanut butter.

Join halves for Chris's favorite sandwich.

4-4-4 Crab Muffins

*When you want to surprise your mother with a
quick and different tasting lunch.*
serves 2

**1 English muffin
4 tablespoons cream cheese
4 tablespoons crab meat, canned
4 tablespoons cocktail sauce**

Cut muffin in half and toast.

Spread each half with 2 tablespoons cream cheese.

Place 2 tablespoons crab on each muffin
and top with cocktail sauce.

Thousand Island Tuna

serves 4

**1 small can tuna fish, drained
⅓ cup Thousand Island dressing
¼ cup peanuts, chopped
1 egg, chopped**

Mix all ingredients together and spread
on toasted bread.

Place lettuce leaf in each sandwich if desired.

Dogs on a Stick

serves 4

4 hot dogs
4 slices bacon
1 (8-ounce) can pineapple chunks
4 skewers

Cut each hot dog and the bacon slices into 3 pieces.

Thread on each skewer a hot dog piece, pineapple chunk, and bacon slice; then repeat.

Place the skewers on cookie sheet and broil for 5 minutes on each side.

Devil Sandwich

serves 4

1 (4½-ounce) can deviled ham
2 hard-cooked eggs, chopped
1 teaspoon horseradish
2 tablespoons diced sweet pickle
1 tablespoon milk

Blend until smooth and spread on your favorite kind of bread. Raisin bread is especially good with this.

Beef

Kima

A Pakistani dish with the flavor of the Orient
serves 4 to 6

1 cup chopped onions
3 tablespoons margarine
1 pound ground beef
¼ teaspoon garlic powder
1 tablespoon curry powder
1½ teaspoons salt
Dash pepper
2 tomatoes, cut up
2 potatoes, cut in very small pieces
1 (10-ounce) package frozen peas
Shredded coconut

Cook onion in margarine over low heat until golden.
Add meat and stir over low heat until lightly browned.

Add all other ingredients.

Cover and simmer for 25 minutes.

Sprinkle with shredded coconut before serving.

Beef Casserole in a Pan

serves 6

1½ pounds ground beef
2 tablespoons minced onions
1 (15-ounce) can macaroni 'n' cheese sauce
1 (8¾-ounce) can whole-kernel corn, drained
1 (4½-ounce) can sliced mushrooms
1 teaspoon salt
½ teaspoon sugar

Brown beef in large frying pan over medium heat.

Stir in minced onions.

Add all other ingredients and heat until boiling.

Cook over very low heat for 15 minutes.

Philip's Hamburger Goulash

serves 4

1½ pounds hamburger
⅛ cup vegetable oil
1 green pepper, chopped
1 (1-pound) can tomatoes
1 (1-pound) can green beans
2 tablespoons minced onions

In vegetable oil, cook hamburger until meat loses its pink color.

Stir in green pepper, tomatoes, green beans and minced onions.

Cook 15 minutes over low heat. Serve over rice or noodles.

Beef

Daddy's Favorite Steak

*I enjoy making this steak and sauce because
everyone loves to eat it. Surprise your father
with this special dinner.*
serves 4

4 small steaks (filet mignon, rib eye, etc.)
Coarsely ground pepper or Lawry's seasoned pepper
½ stick of butter
¼ cup beef broth
⅔ cup heavy cream
½ teaspoon thyme
4 slices bacon, fried and crumbled

Press lots of pepper into both sides of the steak.

Heat heavy iron skillet; add butter.

When butter is melted, brown meat over medium heat
(5 minutes on each side).

Remove steaks.

Turn heat to low and add beef broth to frying pan; stir well.

Simmer for a minute.

Add cream and thyme and let simmer on low heat for a few
minutes. Lastly, add crumbled bacon.

Spoon sauce over steak (and rice, noodles or potato)
and serve.

Five Hour Stew

Make this in the morning and smell the delicious
stew aroma all day.
serves 6

2 pounds of beef stew meat
3 medium onions, chopped
1 cup celery, chopped
6 carrots, chopped
2 cups tomato juice
1 slice bread (broken up)
3 tablespoons tapioca
1 tablespoon sugar
2 teaspoons salt
½ teaspoon pepper
4 potatoes, quartered

Mix all ingredients together and bake in a covered dish
for 5 hours at 250 degrees.

Fancy Dinner Hamburgers

serves 6

2 pounds ground beef
1 package Lipton's onion soup mix
1 teaspoon Worcestershire sauce
1 teaspoon soy sauce
1 teaspoon lemon juice

Mix all ingredients.

Shape meat into patties and broil 5 minutes on each side.

Spaghetti Meat Sauce

*My favorite dinner recipe because it is easy and delicious —
and you can't fail.*
serves 4

⅛ cup salad oil
1½ pounds hamburger
2 cups tomato juice
2 small cans tomato paste
2 tablespoons minced onion
1 teaspoon salt
1 teaspoon pepper
1 teaspoon chili powder
1 teaspoon sugar

Brown meat in salad oil.

Stir in juice, tomato paste, onions, salt, pepper,
chili powder and sugar.

Cook over very low heat for 45 minutes.

Spicy Beef Cakes

serves 4 to 6

1½ pounds ground round
1 egg
½ cup bottled barbecue sauce
½ teaspoon salt
½ teaspoon chili powder

In bowl mix beef, egg, barbecue sauce, salt and chili powder.

Spoon mixture into 6 large muffin pan cups or 6-ounce custard cups.

Bake at 350 degrees for 40 minutes.

Spaghetti Meat Loaf

serves 6

1½ pounds ground beef
1 (1-pound) can spaghetti in tomato sauce
1 egg
1 teaspoon salt
⅛ teaspoon garlic powder
4 slices American cheese
2 tablespoons minced onion

Gently mix ground beef with spaghetti, egg, salt and garlic powder.

Press half the mixture into an 8-by-8-by-2-inch baking pan.

Top with cheese slices and minced onion.

Then spoon remaining beef mixture over all to form loaf.

Bake at 350 degrees for 1 hour.

Six Layer Dinner

serves 4

4 potatoes, sliced
3 onions, sliced
1 (number 2½) can tomatoes, drained
1 pound hamburger
½ cup uncooked rice
4 slices raw bacon

In a large casserole, place potato slices;
next onion slices and tomatoes.

Spread the hamburger on top of the tomatoes.

Sprinkle rice over all and lay bacon on top.

Add cold water to the casserole dish until it reaches
the top of the ingredients.

Cover and bake for 2 hours at 350 degrees.

Chicken

Golden Chicken

serves 4

6 chicken legs (about 2½ pounds)
2 tablespoons melted butter or margarine
1 can golden mushroom soup
¼ cup grape juice
⅛ teaspoon nutmeg
¼ cup pimiento strips

In shallow baking dish, place chicken skin side up.

Pour melted butter over chicken.

Bake at 400 degrees for 40 minutes.

Combine remaining ingredients and spoon over chicken.
Bake 20 minutes more.

Crunchy Oven-Fried Chicken

serves 4

1 (3-pound) ready-to-cook broiler-fryer chicken, cut up
½ cup evaporated milk
1 (4-ounce) package potato chips
1 (4-ounce) package corn chips
½ cup butter, melted
Dash pepper

Dip chicken in milk and roll in crushed chips.

Place in shallow pan, skin side up.

Pour butter over all pieces. Sprinkle lightly
with pepper and bake 1 hour at 375 degrees.

Brown Paper Bag Chicken

Moist chicken every time – lots of finger licking!
serves 2 to 4

1 (2-pound) chicken, ready for roasting
Butter
Stuffing, if desired
1 brown paper bag

Rub entire chicken with butter.

After stuffing chicken (have your mother help you),
close leg and neck openings with string and toothpicks.

Place greased bird in brown paper bag.

Fold opening of bag under.

Place bag in shallow pan and roast at 400 degrees for 2 hours.

Split open bag and chicken is golden brown and ready to eat!

Very Easy Chicken-Rice Casserole

serves 4

1 can mushroom soup
1 can celery soup
1 soup can milk
1 cup uncooked rice
4 chicken breasts
1 package dried onion soup mix

Mix mushroom and celery soups, milk and rice
and pour into a greased casserole dish.

Place chicken on top of soup mixture.

Sprinkle with onion soup mix.

Cover dish with aluminum foil or tight-fitting lid.

Bake at 325 degrees for 2 hours.

Kirstin's Peachy Chicken

serves 6

6 chicken breasts
1 bottle Russian dressing
1 (8-ounce) jar peach preserves
1 package dry onion soup mix

Place breasts in buttered pan.

Mix dressing, preserves and onion soup mix
and pour sauce over chicken. Cover.

Bake for 1½ hours at 350 degrees.

Curry Coconut Chicken

serves 4

1 broiler-fryer, cut up (about 3 pounds)
½ stick of butter or margarine
½ cup honey
¼ cup prepared mustard
1 teaspoon salt
1 teaspoon curry powder
¼ cup shredded coconut

Wash chicken pieces; pat dry.

Melt the butter in a shallow baking pan.

Stir in the remaining ingredients, except coconut.

Roll chicken in butter mixture to coat both sides.

Then arrange skin side up in a single layer in the same pan.

Bake at 375 degrees for 1 hour.

Sprinkle coconut on top before serving.

Honey Barbecued Chicken

serves 4

2 or 3 pounds chicken breasts and thighs
1 egg yolk
1½ teaspoons salt
⅛ teaspoon pepper
1 teaspoon paprika
2 tablespoons soy sauce
1 tablespoon lemon juice
2 tablespoons melted butter
¼ cup honey

Mix all ingredients except chicken together
and dip chicken pieces in sauce.

Lay chicken in pan.

Pour rest of sauce over all.

Bake for 30 minutes at 400 degrees; turn chicken
pieces over and bake for another 40 minutes.

Seafood

Night-Before Crab Casserole

*Before you go to bed make this delicious dinner
and enjoy it the next night!*
serves 6

3 slices bread
2 (6-ounce) cans crab meat, drained
1 cup mayonnaise
1 cup half-and-half
6 hard-cooked eggs, chopped
1 tablespoon minced onion
½ teaspoon salt
½ cup cornflake crumbs

Take crusts off bread and cut into cubes.

Mix crab, mayonnaise, half-and-half, eggs, onion,
salt and bread cubes.

Place in greased casserole dish and put in
refrigerator overnight.

An hour before dinner, sprinkle cornflake crumbs over top
and bake at 350 degrees for 1 hour.

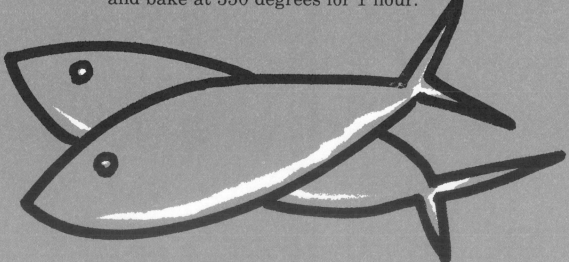

Sole

serves 4

1½ pounds frozen or fresh filet of sole
1 onion, sliced thin
1 cup sour cream
1 teaspoon paprika
½ cup grated Swiss cheese

Place sole (thawed) in greased baking dish.

Cover with onion slices.

Mix sour cream, paprika and cheese together
and pour over fish.

Bake at 375 degrees for 25 minutes.

Hurry Tuna

serves 4

1 can cream of mushroom soup
⅓ cup milk
1 (7-ounce) can tuna, drained
2 hard-cooked eggs, quartered
4 buttered toast slices
4 tablespoons grated Parmesan cheese

In a saucepan, stir over low heat, soup, milk, tuna
and egg quarters.

When hot, spoon mixture over buttered toast and top each
serving with a tablespoon of Parmesan cheese.

Delicious Shrimp Curry

This is very easy to make and more fun to eat!
serves 4

2 (¾-pound) bags frozen shrimp
4 tablespoons butter
4 tablespoons flour
2 cups milk
1 teaspoon salt
6 tablespoons catsup
1 tablespoon curry powder
1 teaspoon paprika

Cook shrimp according to package directions and drain;
set aside.

Melt butter in saucepan over low heat.

Stir in flour until smooth.

Then stir in milk.

Add salt, catsup, curry powder and paprika.

Cook over very low heat for 10 minutes,
stirring occasionally.

Lastly, stir in cooked shrimp and simmer 5 minutes more.

For a special touch, pass small bowls of 2 or 3 of the following:
chopped peanuts, chopped eggs, raisins, chutney,
chopped apple, or chopped onions.

Crab-Apple Quickie

serves 2

1 (6-ounce) can crab meat
1 apple, chopped
1 cup cooked rice
¼ cup milk
¼ cup mayonnaise
½ teaspoon curry powder

Mix all the above ingredients together and place
in small casserole dish.

Bake at 350 degrees for 15 minutes or until heated through.

Crispy Casserole

serves 4 to 6

1 (¾-pound) can shrimp, drained
1 (½-pound) can crab, drained
1 cup mayonnaise
1 cup celery, chopped
1 onion, chopped
1 green pepper, chopped
½ cup corn chip crumbs

Mix shrimp, crab, mayonnaise, celery, onion and green pepper.

Place in buttered casserole.

Sprinkle corn chip crumbs on top.

Bake at 350 degrees for ½ hour.

Fabulous Fish

Different and very good for a special party.
serves 4

1 (6-ounce) can crab meat, drained
1 (6-ounce) can small cocktail shrimp, drained
4 pieces filet of sole
1 (10-ounce) can cheddar cheese soup
4 slices lemon

Mix crab meat and shrimp.

Mound the seafood in the center of each piece
of sole and form roll.

Fasten the rolls with toothpicks holding 1 lemon slice
and a whole shrimp.

Place the rolls in a buttered casserole dish.

Pour soup over all and bake at 400 degrees for 25 minutes.

Sprinkle with paprika and serve.

Pork

Pork Chops with Hawaiian Rice

*I make this often, as "Hawaiian Rice" is one of
my favorite foods.*
serves 4

4 lean loin pork chops
⅛ cup vegetable oil
1 cup water
1 cup uncooked rice
¾ cup green pepper, chopped
1 (15-ounce) can tomato sauce with tidbits
1 (13-ounce) can pineapple chunks, undrained
1 tablespoon vinegar

Heat vegetable oil in large frying pan.

Add pork chops and brown on both sides.

In heavy saucepan, mix water, rice, green pepper, tomato sauce,
undrained pineapple chunks and vinegar.

Place chops on top of rice mixture.

Cook over low heat, tightly covered, for 1 hour.

Corn Dogs

A different kind of hot dog.
serves 4

4 hot dogs
¼ cup catsup
½ cup cornflake crumbs
¼ cup grated cheddar cheese

Roll hot dogs in catsup; then cornflake crumbs.

Sprinkle each dog with grated cheese.

Bake for 15 minutes at 350 degrees.

Choppy Frankfurter Special

serves 4

4 large cooked frankfurters, sliced in ½-inch slices
2 hard-cooked eggs, chopped
1 tablespoon chili sauce
1 tablespoon sweet pickle relish
1 tablespoon chopped parsley
1 teaspoon sesame seeds
1 teaspoon prepared mustard
½ cup grated cheese

Combine all ingredients (except cheese) in a casserole.

Sprinkle top with cheese.

Bake in a preheated 350-degree oven for about 15 minutes.

Ham Quiche

Quiche is easy to prepare and it's so much fun to eat!
serves 4

4 eggs
2 cups lean ham, cooked and diced
8 ounces cottage cheese
1 tablespoon green pepper, chopped
1 teaspoon chives or onion, chopped
½ teaspoon dry mustard
Dash of salt

Beat eggs lightly and stir in remaining ingredients.

Pour mixture into small greased casserole dish and bake in preheated 350-degree oven for about 30 to 45 minutes, or until set like a custard.

Milk-Baked Pork Chops

These pork chops, from a friend in Maine, are so tender
you can cut them with a fork.
serves 4

4 pork chops, ¾-inch thick
4 teaspoons dry mustard
2 cups milk

Place chops in buttered baking dish.

Spread each chop with 1 teaspoon of dry mustard. Pour milk into pan until it reaches top of the chops.

Bake uncovered at 350 degrees for 1½ hours.

Dishes to go with Dinner

Brown Sugar Beans

serves 6

**2 (1-pound) cans baked beans
4 slices bacon
½ cup dark brown sugar**

Empty beans into baking dish.

Top beans with bacon slices.

Sprinkle sugar over all.

Cover and bake at 350 degrees for 30 minutes.

Uncover and continue baking for 30 minutes or until bacon is done.

Oven "French Fries"

serves 4

**4 unpeeled potatoes, washed
2 tablespoons vegetable oil
Paprika**

Cut washed potatoes into ⅓-inch sticks (do not peel).

Toss sticks in salad bowl with vegetable oil.

Place potatoes on greased baking sheet. Sprinkle with paprika and bake at 450 degrees for 8 minutes; then reduce heat to 350 degrees and cook 10 minutes longer.

Honey Rice

serves 6

3 cups cooked rice
½ cup seedless raisins
2½ cups milk
½ cup honey
2 tablespoons butter or margarine
1 teaspoon grated lemon peel
1 tablespoon lemon juice

Combine rice, raisins, milk, honey and butter in saucepan.

Stir in lemon peel and juice.

Bring to boil, reduce heat and cook over low heat uncovered for 15 minutes, stirring occasionally.

Sweet, Sweet Potatoes

serves 6

1 (2½-pound) can dry-pack sweet potatoes
1 stick butter
1 cup milk
½ teaspoon nutmeg
¼ teaspoon cinnamon
¾ cup sugar
1 teaspoon salt

Mash potatoes with all other ingredients. Place in casserole dish. Bake at 325 degrees for 20 minutes, or until glazed on top.

Potato Smash

serves 4

3 cups cooked, sliced potatoes
1 cup cottage cheese
½ cup sour cream
½ cup chopped onions
½ cup grated Parmesan cheese

Stir potatoes, cottage cheese, sour cream and onions together.
Pour into buttered casserole.

Top with grated cheese. Bake at 350 degrees for 30 minutes.

Crusty Noodles

A wonderful and different treat with roast beef or lamb.
serves 6

½ pound thin noodles
1 teaspoon salt
½ stick butter

Cook noodles with salt; drain and rinse in cold water.

Melt butter in iron skillet.

When butter is sizzling hot, add noodles and
stir them around.

Reduce heat and cook very slowly until there is a
light brown crust on bottom of noodles.

Golden Potatoes

serves 4

2 (1-pound) cans small white potatoes
½ can cheddar cheese soup
½ can golden mushroom soup
1 soup can of milk
⅛ teaspoon garlic powder

Drain potatoes.

Place in greased baking dish.

Sprinkle pepper over potatoes.

Mix soups, milk and garlic powder.

Pour this mixture over the potatoes.

Bake, uncovered, at 350 degrees for 45 minutes.

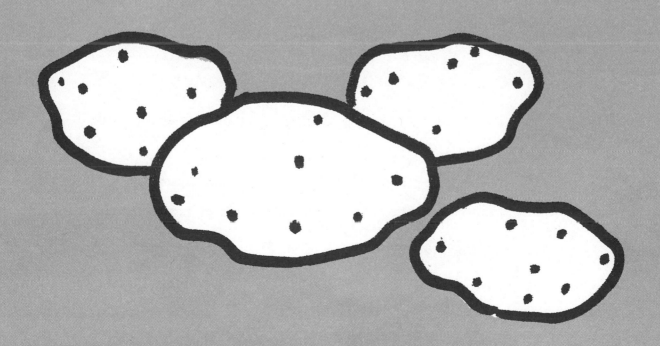

Deviled Baked Potatoes

serves 4

4 baking potatoes
1 small can deviled ham
1 jar of your favorite cheese spread

Scrub potatoes.

Then bake at 450 degrees for 1 hour.

Cut a cross in each potato and top the steaming white inside
with several spoonfuls of deviled ham and a dab of your
favorite cheese sauce (blue cheese is especially good).

Peter's Nutty Turkey Stuffing

serves 6-8

1 package prepared dry stuffing
½ cup chopped Spanish peanuts
½ cup chopped celery

Prepare stuffing according to package directions.

Stir in peanuts and celery.

Place stuffing in turkey.

Vegetables

Corn Pudding

Some people think this pudding is better than chocolate!
serves 4

2 eggs
1 (1-pound) can cream-style corn
1 cup milk
¼ teaspoon black pepper
4 slices white bread
1 slice cooked bacon, crumbled

Beat eggs with rotary beater.

Then add corn, milk, black pepper and bread
(which has been broken into small pieces).

Place bacon bits into greased casserole dish.

Pour in corn mixture. Bake at 350 degrees for 40 minutes.

Creole Green Beans

serves 4

1 (9-ounce) package frozen green beans,
cooked and drained
1 teaspoon minced onion
⅓ cup chili sauce
½ teaspoon salt

Mix in saucepan green beans, onion,
chili sauce and salt.

Cook only until thoroughly heated, stirring often.

Red, Green and Good

serves 6

2 (9-ounce) packages frozen French-style green beans
½ pint cherry tomatoes
2 tablespoons Italian dressing
1 teaspoon garlic salt

Cook green beans according to package directions.

Add tomatoes, dressing and garlic salt.

Heat through and serve.

Vegetable Mix

serves 6

1 (16-ounce) can French-style green beans, drained
1 (16-ounce) can bean sprouts, drained
2 (8-ounce) cans sliced mushrooms, drained
¼ cup grated Parmesan cheese
1 (8-ounce) can tomato sauce
½ teaspoon salt
1 (3½-ounce) can french fried onion rings

Toss together green beans, bean sprouts, mushrooms,
and grated cheese.

Place in covered casserole dish.

Combine tomato sauce and salt and pour over vegetables.

Cover and bake at 350 degrees for 35 minutes.

Uncover dish and sprinkle with french fried
onion rings and bake 10 minutes longer.

Scalloped Onions and Tomatoes

serves 4

¼ cup margarine
1½ cups dry bread crumbs
1½ cups tomatoes (canned or fresh)
3 medium-size onions, sliced very thin
½ teaspoon salt
⅛ teaspoon pepper

Melt the margarine in small saucepan or skillet.

Add bread crumbs and mix well.

In a well-greased baking dish, pour in just enough tomatoes
(about ½ cup) to cover the bottom.

Add a layer of bread-crumb mixture and cover with
a layer of thinly sliced onions. Sprinkle with salt and pepper.

Then repeat: a layer of tomatoes, bread crumbs
and onions (the top layer should be bread crumbs).
Bake at 375 degrees for 40 minutes.

Quick-As-A-Wink Spinach

serves 6

2 (10-ounce) packages frozen spinach, cooked and drained
2 teaspoons minced onion
⅓ cup sour cream
1 tablespoon prepared horseradish
½ teaspoon salt

Combine all ingredients in a saucepan.

Cook over low heat until hot (about 5 minutes).

Magic-Six Tomatoes

*When you add 6 ingredients to these tomatoes,
they are delicious!*
serves 4

**2 large tomatoes
1 teaspoon sugar
Salt
Pepper
½ teaspoon garlic powder
4 thin slices of onion
2 tablespoons grated Parmesan cheese**

Cut tomatoes in half.

For each tomato half do 6 things: sprinkle with
¼ teaspoon sugar, dash of salt, dash of pepper,
⅛ teaspoon garlic powder, thin slice of onion
and ½ tablespoon grated cheese.

Place in 500-degree oven for 5 minutes.

Black Bananas

Hot, black-skinned bananas are fun to serve.
serves 4

**4 unpeeled, ripe bananas
Vegetable shortening**

Grease bananas with shortening.

Place on cookie tin and bake for 30 minutes
(or until almost black) at 300 degrees.

Serve in their skins.

Santa Cruz Casserole

serves 4

1 (16-ounce) can tomatoes, drained
1 (12-ounce) can whole kernel corn
½ cup green pepper, chopped
¼ cup onions, chopped
½ teaspoon salt
¼ teaspoon pepper
2 tablespoons melted butter
¼ cup seasoned bread crumbs
¼ cup grated Parmesan cheese

Combine first 6 ingredients in a casserole dish.

Mix butter, bread crumbs and cheese and
sprinkle over top of casserole.

Bake 20 minutes in preheated 400-degree oven.

Milky Way Peas

serves 6

½ cup milk
2 (10-ounce) packages frozen peas
2 tablespoons butter
½ teaspoon sugar

Heat milk.

Add frozen peas and stir until peas and milk are well mixed.

Cook over low heat for 5 minutes.

Stir in butter and sugar and serve.

Desserts

Liz Ann's Butterscotch Brownies

*Liz Ann makes these special brownies whenever she gets
a chance. They are wonderful!*
yield: 35

2 cups (12-ounce package) butterscotch bits
½ cup brown sugar
½ cup margarine
2 eggs
1½ cups all-purpose flour
2 teaspoons baking powder
½ teaspoon salt
2 teaspoons vanilla
2 cups (12-ounce package) semisweet chocolate bits
2 cups miniature marshmallows
1 cup chopped pecans

In large saucepan melt butterscotch pieces, sugar and
margarine over medium heat, stirring constantly.

Remove from heat.

Add eggs and beat well.

Sift flour, baking powder and salt together.
Add to egg mixture.

Finally, stir in vanilla, chocolate pieces,
marshmallows and pecans.

Spread in 10-by-15-inch greased pan.

Bake at 350 degrees for 20 to 25 minutes.

When cool, cut into bars.

Chocolate Mint Pudding

When "just chocolate" won't do.
serves 4

1 package chocolate pudding mix
5 (3-inch) peppermint sticks

Cook pudding according to package directions.

As mix cooks, drop 1 peppermint stick, broken into small pieces, into mix.

When pudding is thick, pour into 4 dishes and top each with a peppermint stick.

Red, White and Blue Sundae

serves 1

1 large scoop raspberry sherbet
1 small scoop vanilla ice cream
½ cup blueberries
1 tablespoon whipped cream
1 cherry

Place raspberry scoop on plate.

Top with slightly smaller scoop of vanilla ice cream.

Add blueberries, whipped cream and cherry.

Happy July 4th!

Chocolate Chip-Nut Pie

serves 8

1 cup sugar
½ cup flour
2 eggs, slightly beaten
1 stick butter or margarine, melted and cooled
1 cup English walnuts, broken
1 cup chocolate chips
1 teaspoon vanilla
1 unbaked pie shell

Mix sugar and flour.

Add eggs, melted butter, walnuts, chocolate chips and vanilla.

Pour into unbaked pie shell and bake in preheated
325-degree oven for one hour.

Test with toothpick before removing from oven to be sure
filling is not runny.

Strawberry Pie

serves 6

1 cooked pie shell
1 (3-ounce) package strawberry gelatin
1 cup boiling water
1 (10-ounce) box frozen strawberries

Melt gelatin in the boiling water. Then add frozen strawberries
and stir until ice dissolves. Let stand for 10 minutes. Pour
into pie shell and chill 2 hours until firm.

Jane's Quick Indian Pudding

serves 4

⅔ cup Instant Cream of Wheat
2½ cups milk
¼ cup molasses
½ teaspoon cinnamon
¼ cup sugar

Place cream of wheat, milk, molasses, cinnamon and sugar
in saucepan. Stir constantly over low heat until mixture
forms bubbles. Let boil for ½ minute.

Remove from heat and pour into dessert dishes. Serve warm
with cream or vanilla ice cream.

Blizzard Cake

*This cake is lots of fun to decorate,
and you can do it by yourself.*
serves 10

1 package white cake mix
1 can chocolate frosting
2 cups popped corn

Bake cake according to package instructions.

Cool.

Ice with chocolate frosting and cover entire cake with a
blizzard of popcorn snowflakes.

Peach Crumbly

serves 6

2 (#2) cans sliced peaches, drained
1 stick pie crust mix
1 (2½-ounce) package slivered almonds
1 cup brown sugar
Butter

Place peaches in shallow baking dish.

Mix pie crust mix, nuts and sugar.

Sprinkle over peaches.

Dot generously with butter and bake at 325 degrees
for 30 minutes.

Serve with cream or vanilla ice cream.

Peanut Butter Pudding

serves 4

1 package vanilla instant pudding
¼ cup crunchy peanut butter
4 tablespoons marshmallow topping

Prepare pudding as directed.

Beat in peanut butter with a rotary beater.

Spoon pudding into dessert dishes. Top with marshmallow
and chill in refrigerator for 1 hour.

All Kinds of Snowballs

*These are almost as much fun to make as real snowballs —
and taste better besides.*

**Vanilla ice cream
Coconut, flaked or shredded
Sauce (chocolate, caramel, butterscotch, strawberry
or pineapple)**

With an ice cream scoop, form balls of vanilla ice cream.

Roll in coconut.

Place on cookie sheet in freezer until firm.

Serve with favorite sauce.

Just Strawberries

serves 1

**⅛ cup brown sugar
⅛ cup sour cream (or yogurt)
½ dozen whole strawberries, with stems and leaves**

Put brown sugar and sour cream side by side in center of a
large dessert plate.

Surround by strawberries.

To eat, hold berry by stem and dip first in sour cream;
then in sugar.

As Easy as Eating Homemade Ice Cream

Once you make this ice cream, you'll be a hero to your family and friends. And there's no cooking.
serves 10

6 eggs
1½ cups sugar
2 cartons half-and-half
3½ pints whipping cream
Rock salt
Crushed ice

Beat eggs till foamy.

Add sugar and beat again for a minute.

Add half-and-half and cream.

Beat 2 minutes until well mixed.

Pour into ice cream container, cover tightly and place in freezer tub. Pack one-third of the freezer with ice and add layers of salt and ice around the container until the freezer is full.

For vanilla ice cream: add 3 tablespoons vanilla.

For chocolate: add 1 can Hershey's fudge topping.

(Mix flavorings in before freezing.)

Cookies

Circus Cookies

yield: 5½ dozen

1 cup butter or margarine
1½ cups brown sugar
3 cups sifted flour
½ teaspoon salt
½ teaspoon soda
2 eggs
2 teaspoons vanilla
2 cups peanuts
Sugar

Cream butter and brown sugar.

Sift flour, salt and soda together.

Add eggs, vanilla and sifted dry ingredients
to butter and sugar mixture.

Stir in peanuts.

Shape into balls about the size of a walnut. Place
about 2 inches apart on ungreased cookie sheet.

Flatten with a fork to about ⅓ inch.
Sprinkle with granulated sugar.

Bake in a 350-degree oven for 12 to 15 minutes.

Hopscotch Jumbles

yield: 2 ½ dozen

½ cup peanut butter
1 (6-ounce) package butterscotch bits
1 (3-ounce) can chow mein noodles
1 cup miniature marshmallows

Melt peanut butter and butterscotch bits in double boiler over hot water. Remove from heat.

Stir in noodles and marshmallows.

Drop by teaspoonfuls onto waxed paper. Chill until set.

Mexican Wedding Cake Cookies

yield: 4 dozen

1 cup butter
¼ cup powdered sugar
1 teaspoon vanilla
2 cups sifted flour
1 cup chopped nuts

Beat butter and sugar until light.

Add vanilla and flour and mix well.

Stir in nuts.

Shape into balls and flatten to ¼-inch thickness.

Bake in 325-degree oven for 20 minutes.

Roll in more powdered sugar while cookies are still hot.

Graham Cracker Sandwiches

These sandwiches are fun to make.
serves 1

1 thin slice of raw apple
2 graham crackers
¼ of a flat chocolate bar
1 marshmallow

Put apple slice on a cracker, then chocolate and marshmallow.

Place on cookie sheet and place in 500-degree oven. Watch carefully until marshmallow starts to turn brown. Remove from oven.

Top with another graham cracker. Press down until the marshmallow goes squish into the melted chocolate.

Hidden Treasure Cookies

It's what's inside that's good.
yield: 1½ dozen

1 roll refrigerated sugar cookie dough
2 chocolate peanut bars

Cut cookie dough into ¼-inch slices.

For each hidden cookie place piece of candy on a cookie slice and top with another cookie.

Press edges together.

Bake on ungreased cookie sheet for 8 to 10 minutes.

Cornflake Cookies

yield: 3 dozen

½ cup butter or margarine
½ cup granulated sugar
½ cup brown sugar, firmly packed
1 egg
1 cup sifted all-purpose flour
1½ teaspoons baking powder
¼ teaspoon salt
1 cup shredded coconut
1 cup cornflakes

Cream butter with sugars.

Beat egg into mixture.

Sift flour, baking powder and salt and add to batter.

Stir in coconut and cornflakes.

Drop by level tablespoons 2 inches apart on
ungreased cookie sheet.

Bake in 350-degree oven for about 10 minutes.
Cool slightly before removing from cookie sheet.

Somemores

*This cookie has been a favorite of campers,
including me, for many, many years.*
serves 1

1 banana
2 squares sweet chocolate
1 caramel, cut in half
6 miniature marshmallows

Split banana so that you can fill it with the chocolate,
caramel and marshmallows. Then wrap banana in tin
foil and bake for 5 minutes at 400 degrees (or until
candies are melted).

Great dessert for a picnic.

No Bake Cookie Balls

yield: 4 dozen

2 cups sugar
¼ cup cocoa
½ cup milk
1 stick butter
½ cup peanut butter
1 teaspoon vanilla
3 cups rolled oats

Combine sugar, cocoa and milk in pan and boil for one minute.

Add remaining ingredients and roll into balls.

Eat!

Gumdrop Cookies

Lots of stirring, rolling, squishing and eating!
yield: 4 dozen

½ cup butter
½ cup granulated sugar
½ cup brown sugar
2 eggs
1 cup, plus 2 tablespoons flour
½ teaspoon baking powder
½ teaspoon baking soda
¼ teaspoon salt
1 cup spiced gumdrops, cut in small pieces
1 cup uncooked cornflakes
½ cup moist coconut

Cream butter and sugars and add eggs. Sift flour, baking powder, soda and salt and add to butter and sugar mixture. Stir in remaining ingredients. Chill in refrigerator.

Roll in round balls, about the size of walnuts.

Place on cookie sheet and flatten slightly with a fork.

Bake in 350-degree oven until light brown, but not hard, about 10 minutes.

Skillet Cookies

yield: 3 dozen

⅓ cup butter
2 eggs
1 cup sugar
1 cup chopped dates
2 cups Rice Crispies
Coconut or finely chopped nuts

Melt butter in skillet.

Beat eggs until foamy; add sugar and stir well.
Pour into skillet.

Add chopped dates.

Cook about 15 minutes over very low heat,
stirring frequently as mixture bubbles.

Let stand until lukewarm. Stir in Rice Crispies.

Form into balls about the size of a walnut and roll
in coconut or chopped nuts.

Store in tight tin box.

Foods from Famous Friends

Mister Rogers' Snow Pudding

Everyone on television's "Mister Rogers' Neighborhood" loves "Snow Pudding." It tastes good but most of all it is fun to prepare. Mr. Rogers describes how he makes snow you can eat: "Presto! An egg white so clear you can see through it plops into the mixing bowl and in just a minute an egg beater whips it into a fluffy mountain." Add the other ingredients and the fluffy mountain tastes different from any snow that has ever melted in your mouth!

serves 6 to 8

¾ cup sugar
1 tablespoon unflavored gelatin (1 envelope)
1¼ cups water
½ cup lemon juice
1 tablespoon grated lemon rind
2 egg whites

Mix together sugar, gelatin and water in saucepan.

Stir constantly, while bringing to a boil.

Blend in lemon juice and rind.

Place pan in cold water and cool until mixture mounds when dropped from a spoon.

Beat egg whites until stiff.

Using rotary beater, slowly blend gelatin mixture into beaten egg whites.

After blending, stir mixture with rubber spatula until it holds its shape.

Spoon into dessert dishes or mold and chill until firm.

Makes 6 to 8 servings.

Captain Kangaroo's Banana Delight

Bob Keeshan, beloved by children as Captain Kangaroo, has many young friends who enjoy making his favorite recipe, "Banana Delight." The recipe is originally from southern Germany, although the graham cracker crust is a substitute for some crispy, sweet German wafers which are unavailable in the United States. "Banana Delight" is simple to prepare and makes a delicious dessert.

Graham Cracker Crust

Combine 2 cups graham cracker crumbs and 6 tablespoons melted butter.

Filling

**1 cup butter
2 cups confectioners' sugar
3 eggs
1 teaspoon vanilla
4 or 5 large bananas — sliced — not combined with above**

Cream butter. Add sugar gradually.

Add eggs, one at a time. Add vanilla.

Pat graham cracker crumbs into a 9-by-13-inch pan.

Pour filling in. Place bananas on top.

Topping

**2 cups heavy cream
¼ cup sugar
1 teaspoon vanilla**

Beat all three ingredients until fluffy.

Put this "whipped cream" combination on top of bananas. Refrigerate overnight.

Maria von Trapp's Kaiserschmarren

Maria von Trapp, the real Maria of The Sound of Music, *has enjoyed Kaiserschmarren for many years. As a child, it was her favorite food whenever she was ill. She describes it as "from the pancake family, very light and very good."*
It tastes best when served with Preisselbeeren, an Austrian cousin of the American cranberry, but your favorite jam will do nicely!
serves 8

1 cup flour
Pinch of salt
1 tablespoon sugar
2 teaspoons baking powder
3 eggs
⅔ to 1 cup milk
¾ stick of butter
⅓ cup raisins

Sift flour, salt, sugar and baking powder into bowl.

Beat eggs slightly and add ⅔ cup milk.

Pour eggs and milk into dry ingredients and stir to blend.

If batter is thick, add more milk to thin.

Melt 1½ tablespoons butter in a 6- or 7-inch pan or skillet over medium heat.

Pour in half the batter.

Sprinkle half of the raisins on top and cook until golden brown on underside.

Lift the edges with a pancake turner while cooking and tilt the skillet a little to permit the uncooked portion to run to the bottom of the pan.

When most of moisture on top is gone, add another 1½ tablespoons of butter, turn the omelette over and cook until golden brown on the other side as well.

Cook second half of batter the same as the first.

With two forks, tear omelette into little pieces and allow to become almost dry.

Serve with stewed cranberries (or your favorite jam).

Clare Boothe Luce's French Toast

French toast was one of Clare Luce's favorite foods as a child. She writes, "It was my busy mother's favorite dish too because I could make it myself and so could my brother." In addition to breakfast, it can be served as a luncheon dish, sprinkled with brown or powdered sugar. And it also can be served as a dessert, with your favorite cookies, fruits or jam.
serves 1

1 egg
¼ cup milk
Dash salt
1 teaspoon sugar
2 slices bread, with crusts removed

Beat egg well.

Stir in milk, salt and sugar.

Soak the bread in the egg mixture for one minute.

Put one pat of butter in a frying pan, over low heat.

Just before butter turns brown, carefully lift bread from bowl,
place in pan and fry on both sides over medium heat
until bread is light golden brown.

Lynda Johnson Robb's Play Cookies

Lynda Robb and her daughters Cindy and Kathy love to make pretend cookies. They use them for beautiful tree ornaments or as Christmas cards, with messages painted by the girls. The cookies are beautiful to look at but you can't eat them!

**2 parts flour to
1 part salt
Enough water to make a "dough"
Water color paints or magic markers**

Roll out the play dough; cut into shapes and bake at
350 degrees until hard.

When cool, color with paints or magic markers.

Mamie Eisenhower's Turkey with Sauerkraut Stuffing

*When Mamie Doud Eisenhower was growing up, first in
Boone, Iowa and later in Denver, Colorado, Thanksgivings and
Christmases were special family celebrations. The Doud turkey
was always stuffed with sauerkraut! As Mamie says,
"it gives the bird a whole new flavor — and it's easy."*

**One turkey, any size desired
Canned sauerkraut, drained (number of cans depending
on amount needed for bird)**

Prepare the bird for stuffing by removing giblets.

Loosely fill both neck and body cavities
with drained sauerkraut.

Close openings, using toothpicks and string.

Brush surface of turkey with vegetable oil and roast at
325 degrees approximately 20 minutes per pound.

For best results use a meat thermometer. Make a small gash
with a knife and then insert thermometer between the thigh and
the body of the bird, taking care that tip of thermometer
does not touch the bone.

Mrs. Billy Graham's Tsao Fan: "Chinese Fried Rice, Ham and Eggs"

Ruth Graham, the daughter of missionary parents, grew up in China. One of the highlights of her childhood was the yearly train ride to Shanghai. The best part of the trip was the "Tsao Fan" served in the dining car: fried ham and scrambled eggs, mixed with fried rice. Today, it is a favorite meal of the Graham children. Mrs. Graham writes, "Bowls and chopsticks are a must!"

serves 4

2 cups cold cooked rice
2 tablespoons salad oil
2 to 3 slices ham
2 eggs, beaten
2 tablespoons soy sauce

Cook rice in oil over medium heat until golden colored, stirring constantly.

Cut 2 slices of ham into small pieces and cook in butter until golden.

Add to rice.

Finally, add beaten eggs to rice-ham mixture and stir over medium heat until egg is set — about 10 seconds.

Instead of salt, sprinkle soy sauce over all, if desired.

Barbara Walters' Brownies

Barbara Walters' favorite dish as a child was her mother's stuffed cabbage but her own daughter Jacqueline's favorite is brownies. These special brownies keep well, if you don't eat them all at one or two sittings!
yield: 16

2½ squares unsweetened chocolate
⅓ cup shortening
1 cup granulated sugar
2 eggs, well beaten
½ cup self-rising flour
½ cup chopped walnuts
1 teaspoon vanilla

Preheat oven to 375 degrees.

Melt chocolate and shortening together.

Add sugar to the well-beaten eggs.

Combine the mixtures.

Sift flour into the mixture.

Add nuts and vanilla. Blend.

Spread the dough evenly in a greased square 8-by-8-by-2-inch pan.

Bake for 20 to 25 minutes.

When cool, cut into squares or bars.

Julie Andrews' Oatmeal Cookies

*What does the fabulous Mary Poppins eat when she is
hungry for a snack? Oatmeal cookies have been
Julie Andrews' favorites for a long time. Today she
bakes them often for her children and their friends.
An added bonus is that the cookies are, in her words, "very healthy."*
yield: 2 dozen

2 sticks butter or margarine, melted
½ cup brown sugar, packed in cup
4 tablespoons molasses
5 cups quick-cooking rolled oats

Mix melted butter with the brown sugar and molasses.

Add the oats and mix. If too moist, add more oats.

Press into a greased 9-by-13-inch baking pan and bake at
350 degrees 15 to 20 minutes.

Cut in pan before cooling.

Mike Douglas' Mother's Golden Baked Chicken

Mike Douglas claims that "as children, when we sat down to eat one of Mom's meals we never left anything on our plates . . . because everything she made tasted so good."
Without a doubt you will enjoy Mother Dowd's easy-to-prepare chicken.
serves 6

2 pounds chicken parts
¼ cup flour
½ teaspoon paprika
½ teaspoon salt
⅛ teaspoon pepper
¼ cup melted butter
1 (10¼-ounce) can undiluted cream of chicken soup
½ cup of water
1 tablespoon minced parsley

Roll chicken in flour and seasonings.

Melt butter over low heat in shallow baking dish.

Arrange chicken in a single layer, skin side down, in baking dish.

Bake at 375 degrees for 20 minutes; turn chicken; bake 20 minutes longer.

Blend soup and water. Pour over chicken.

Sprinkle top with parsley.

Bake 20 minutes longer.

Honey Bananas

•

by Caroll Spinney

a favorite recipe from BIG BIRD's kitchen!

You'll need two bananas, honey and butter.

① Slice the bananas into two pieces, like this.

② Melt a little butter in a frying-pan-medium heat.

Put the bananas in!

Now put a strip of honey on the top side of each banana!

③

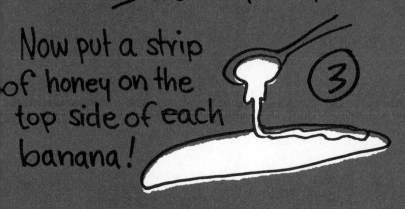

④ Just cook one minute each side! Yummy alone or with eggs or anything!

Frank Sinatra's Queen Cakes

The Sinatra family has always been close-knit, and Frank Sinatra has many happy memories of family times together in the kitchen. When he was nine years old, his grandmother taught him how to make Queen Cakes. Through the years he has loved these easy-to-prepare cakes that you bake in paper cups.
yield: 2½ dozen

½ pound butter or margarine
1 cup sugar
2 small eggs
⅔ cup half-and-half
2 cups flour
1½ cups currants
Paper cups

Place the butter and sugar in a mixing bowl and beat until smooth and creamy. Beat in eggs, one at a time.

Mix in half and half.

Stir in flour and currants, mixing well.

Spoon mixture into paper cups, filling each only halfway.

Bake 20 minutes at 350 degrees, or until golden.

When cool you may ice these with your favorite icing.